LOOK INSIDE

Trainer

Catherine Chambers

Heinemann
LIBRARY

First published in Great Britain by Heinemann Library
Halley Court, Jordan Hill, Oxford OX2 8EJ
a division of Reed Educational and Professional Publishing Ltd
Heinemann is a registered trademark of Reed Educational and Professional
Publishing Limited.

OXFORD FLORENCE PRAGUE MADRID ATHENS
MELBOURNE AUCKLAND KUALA LUMPUR SINGAPORE TOKYO
IBADAN NAIROBI KAMPALA JOHANNESBURG GABORONE
PORTSMOUTH NH CHICAGO MEXICO CITY SAO PAULO

Designed by Celia Floyd
Printed in Hong Kong

02 01 00 99 98
10 9 8 7 6 5 4 3 2 1

ISBN 0 431 08680 X

British Library Cataloguing in Publication Data

Chambers, Catherine
  Trainer. – (Look inside)
  1. Athletic shoes – Juvenile literature 2. Athletic shoes –
  Design and construction – Juvenile literature
  I. Title
  685.3'102

Acknowledgements
The Publisher would like to thank the following for permission to reproduce photographs:
Chris Honeywell, pp.4–21

Cover photograph: Chris Honeywell

Our thanks to Betty Root for her comments in the preparation of this book and to CICA for
their assistance.

Every effort has been made to contact copyright holders of any material reproduced in this
book. Any omissions will be rectified in subsequent printings if notice is given to the Publisher.

CONTENTS

Some words are shown in bold, **like this**. You can find out what they mean by looking in the glossary.

HERE'S A TRAINER

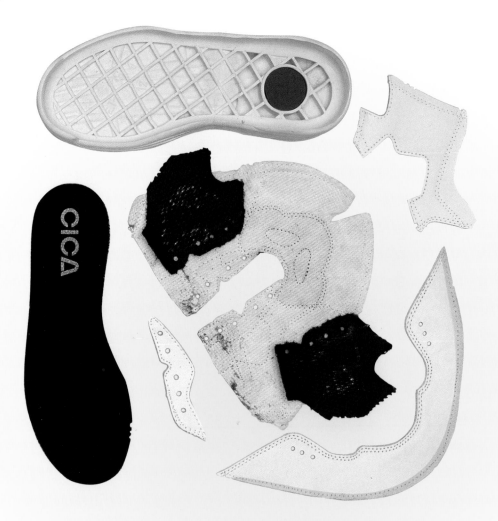

Look at these bits and pieces. Some are large. Others are tiny. Some are soft and spongy. Others are tough and **flexible**, or hard and strong.

Now look at the shapes of the pieces. Most of them are rounded. Some lie flat. Others stay curved. But they all fit together to make a strong, comfortable trainer. How is it done?

LONG LACES

Laces are long and thin. They pull the sides of the shoe together. But there's still some left to tie a bow. The material is loosely **woven**, so it stretches without snapping.

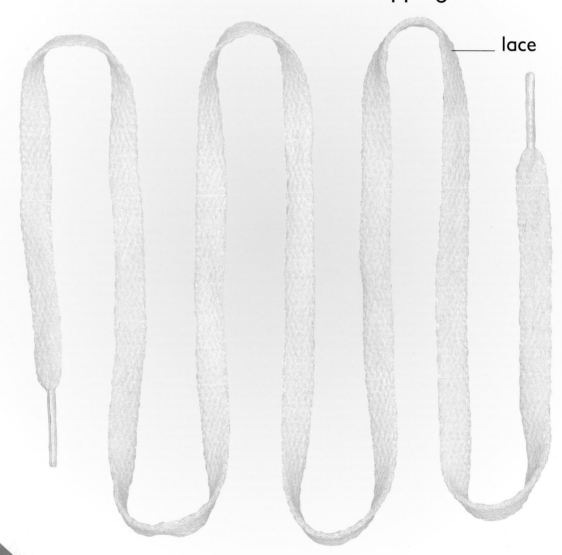

_____ lace

A piece of hard plastic is squeezed round the ends of each lace. This stops the lace from **fraying**. It also makes the laces easier to thread through the eyelets.

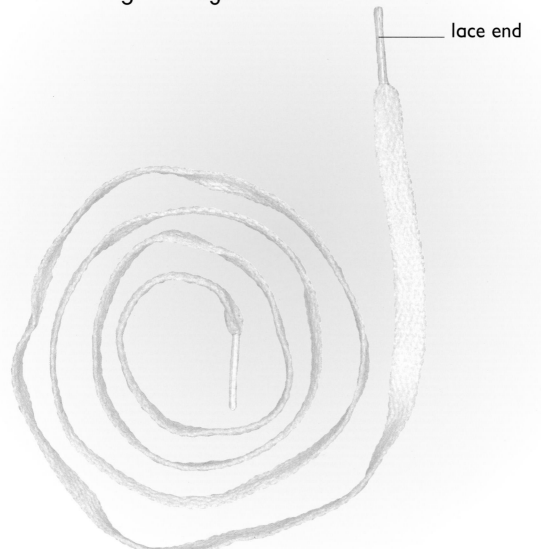

lace end

THE EYELETS

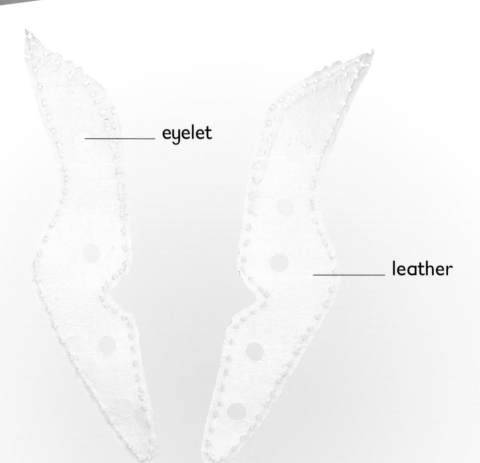

eyelet

leather

The eyelets are holes punched into two pieces of leather. The leather is strong and **flexible**. It doesn't tear when the laces are pulled through the eyelets. The leather is also soft, so it doesn't tear the laces.

8

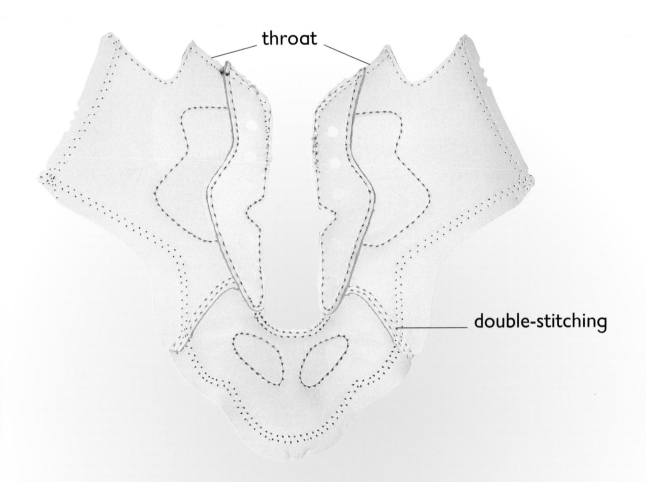

throat

double-stitching

The two pieces of leather are stitched to
three others. This is then called the throat.
Strong thread is used. Two rows of stitches
are sewn where extra strength is needed.
This is called double-stitching.

HEELS AND TOES

The heel and toe are rounded, like the shape of your foot. The shape of the toe and heel let the foot bend. So does the **flexible** leather. They also **support** the foot.

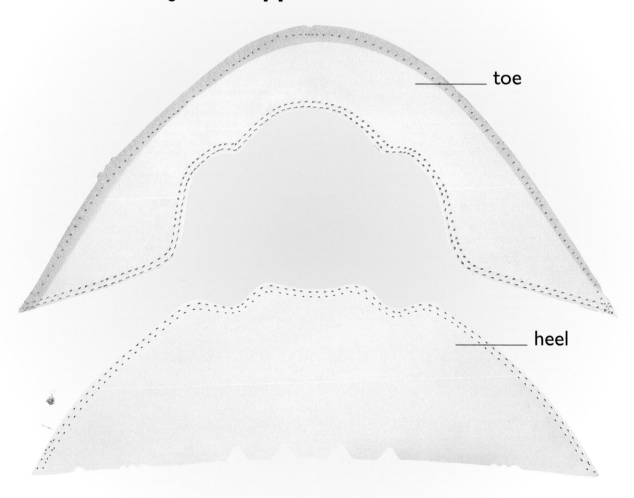

toe

heel

The heel has to be extra strong. It gets a lot of wear. So it is stiffened with a hard **thermo-plastic**. The heel and toe are then stitched to the throat. The whole piece is called the upper.

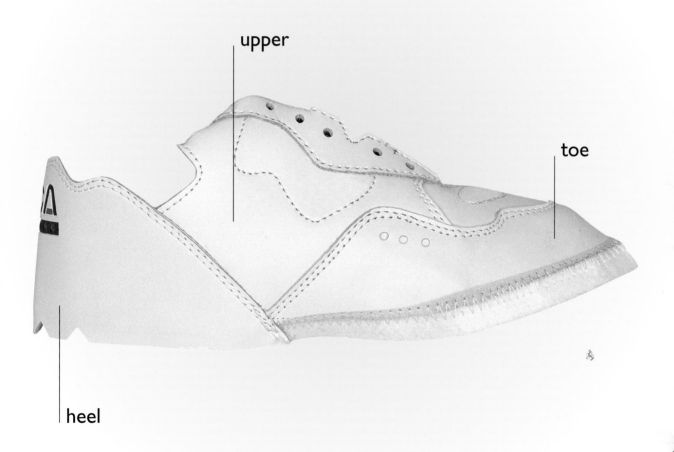

upper

toe

heel

PATTERNS AND COLOURS

The leather must look good. It must also be protected. These pieces of leather have a white coating. This can be wiped clean and then polished. Red and black **logos** are pressed into the leather.

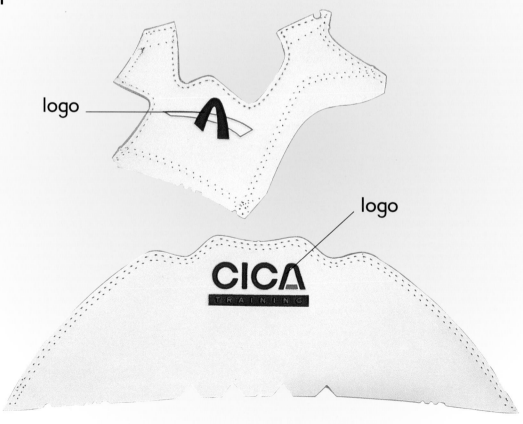

logo

logo

CICA
TRAINING

Black and red patterns are made from **woven synthetic** material. They are sewn into holes cut into the leather. These are stitched onto the uppers with the rest of the liners.

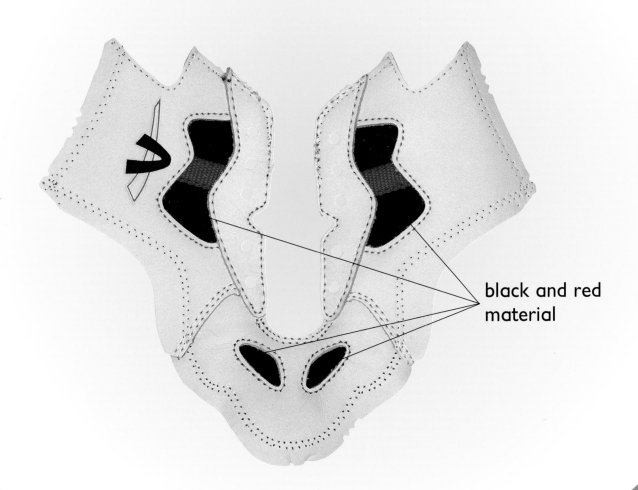

black and red material

THE LINERS

Liners are stitched inside the shoe. Your foot fits right next to the liners, so they have to be comfortable. Liners are made from **synthetic** material. They are thin and soft. But they are strong, too.

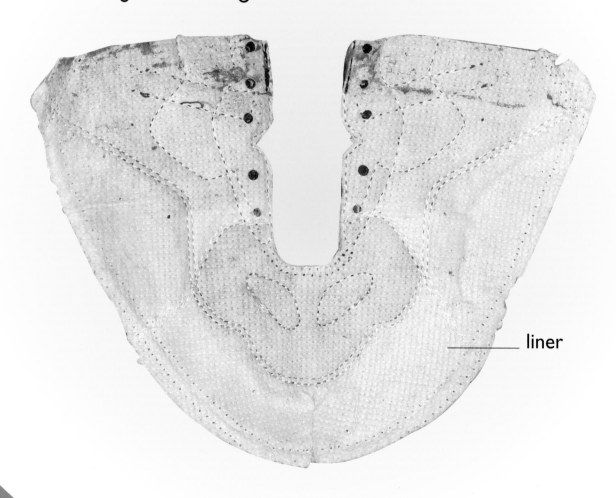

_____ liner

Soft fabric and spongy filler are used on the tongue and around the heel. This stops them from rubbing against your foot. A label with a **logo** is stitched to the tongue. Now they're ready for the soles.

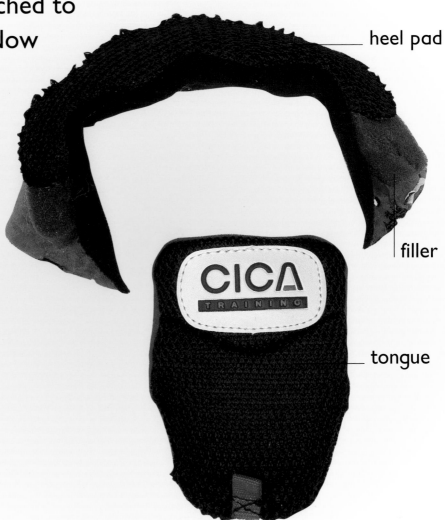

heel pad

filler

tongue

STRONG SOLES

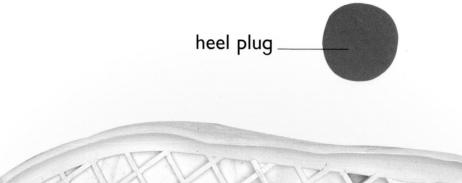

heel plug ———

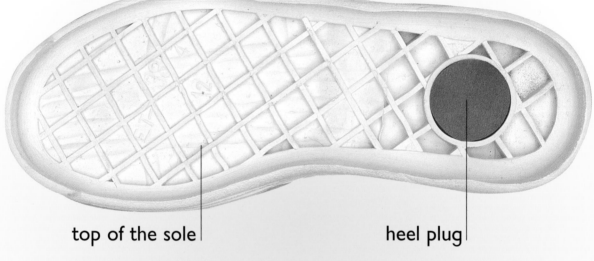

top of the sole

heel plug

Soles are moulded from **polyurethane**. This makes them thick and springy. It also makes them tough but **flexible**. The blue heel plug disc is made of polyurethane foam. It protects the heel when you jump or run. It **absorbs** the shock.

The top of the sole is flat. This is where your foot rests. But the underneath is **grooved**. This helps the sole to grip the ground. The soles are sealed onto the uppers with a cement. A powerful **pressure-lasting** process is used.

grooves

underneath the sole

CICA

INSOCKS AND INSOLES

Insocks are stuck on top of the sole, where your foot rests. They are made from off-cuts of leather. These are the pieces left over from making the uppers. The leather is made into a **pulp**. It is then pressed, dried and cut into the shape of your foot.

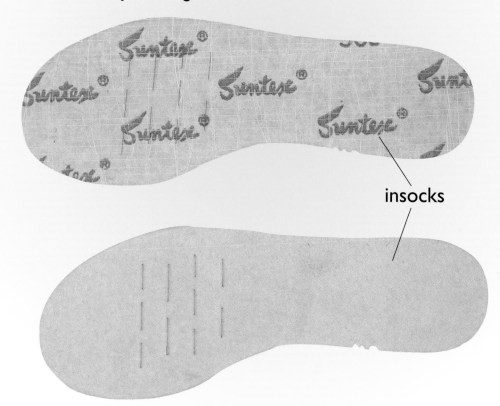

insocks

The trainer is still a bit hard inside. It needs soft, springy insoles. These are made from **polyurethane** foam. A tough, stretchy material is stuck on top.

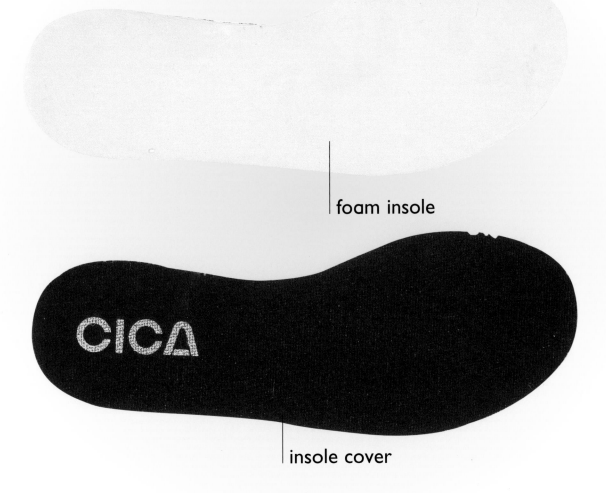

foam insole

CICA

insole cover

LET'S WALK!

So here are the trainers. All the bits and pieces have been put together. There are other kinds of trainers, too. Some have plastic bubbles in the soles. Or flashing lights. Some trainers even glow in the dark. Others pump up if you press the tongue!

The patterns and decorations don't matter. All trainers are tough, springy, bendy, comfy and trendy. You can run in them. You can play in them. They're fun. But they're good for your feet, too.

GLOSSARY

absorbs   soaks up

flexible   bends easily

fraying   when a material wears away and breaks at the ends

grooved   cut with deep lines

logos   symbols used to show who made something

polyurethane   a synthetic material

pressure-lasting   stuck together with great force by machine

pulp   a mashed up material mixed with a liquid

support   to hold firmly

synthetic   made by people, not natural

thermo-plastic   a hardened synthetic material

woven   when threads are crossed over each other to make a material

Further reading

How it's made: Shoes. Ruth Thomson. Watts, 1993

Making... Shoes. Ruth Thomson. Watts, 1986

New Shoes. Kate Petty. A&C Black, 1991

Our Clothes: Leather Shoes. Wayne Jackman. Wayland, 1990

INDEX